Teacher Swears

Swear Word Coloring Book to
Rant & Relax

By
I ♥ Coloring Books

Introduction

Irreverent sayings for Teachers fill the following pages. They are meant for entertainment purposes for grownups only so don't get bent out of shape about them.

Sometimes after a long hard day of dealing with the little darlings, their parents, and the administration, you just need to chill out. To sit back with your beverage of choice and color the things you really want to say to all those people who got on your last nerve today, and if you can learn a few new "choice phrases" so much the better!

Teacher Swears is the perfect way to unwind and release your inner potty mouth. Enjoy these irreverent, yet beautiful adult coloring pages. Then sit back and sigh after a job well done.

These single sided pages range from moderate to highly detailed and include abstract patterns, animals, flowers and more… Each has its own cleverly coded swear that, while not necessarily appropriate for the classroom will definitely relieve stress in the break room! Sayings like "Holy Cheeseballs," "Zip it Happy Meal," and my personal favorite, "F.O.C.U.S. People!" (standing for F*ck Off Cuz' Ur Stupid!).

You'll find these and 22 other humorous, subversive sayings to expand your inappropriate vocabulary and help you de-stress and relax!

Enjoy!

I ♥ Coloring Books

Color Test Page

Color Test Page

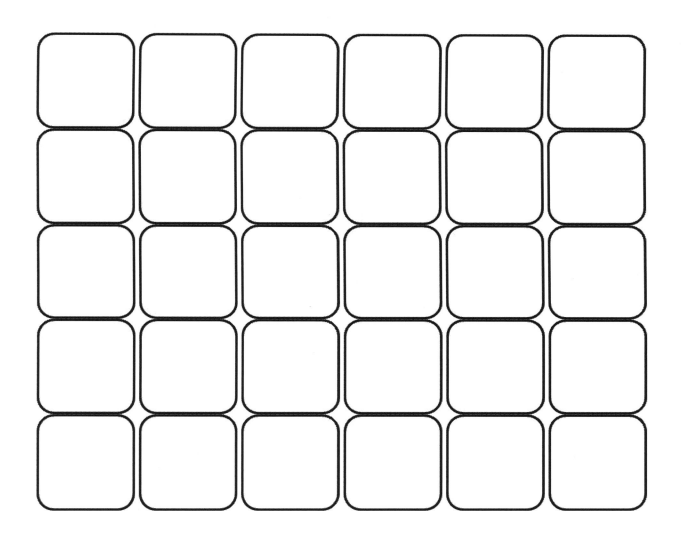

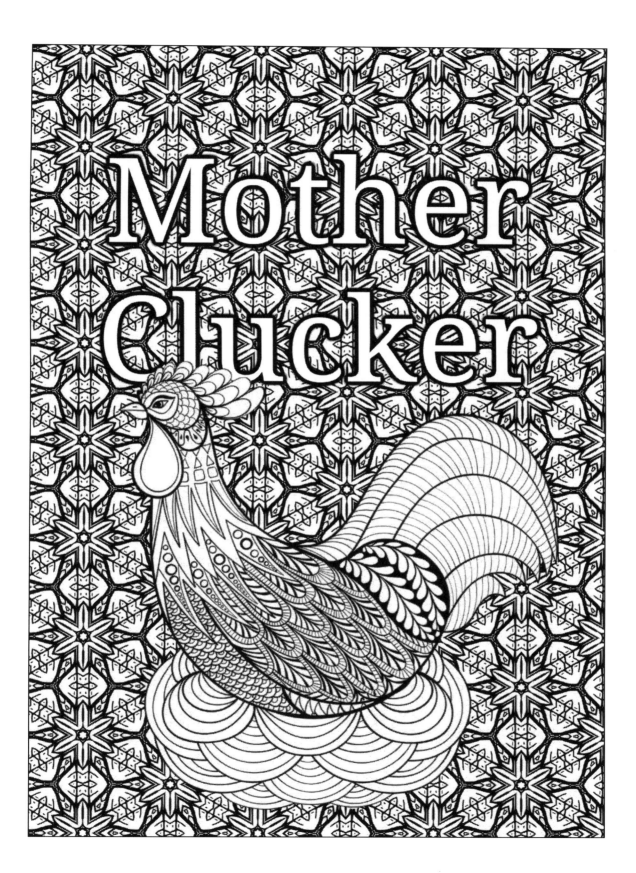

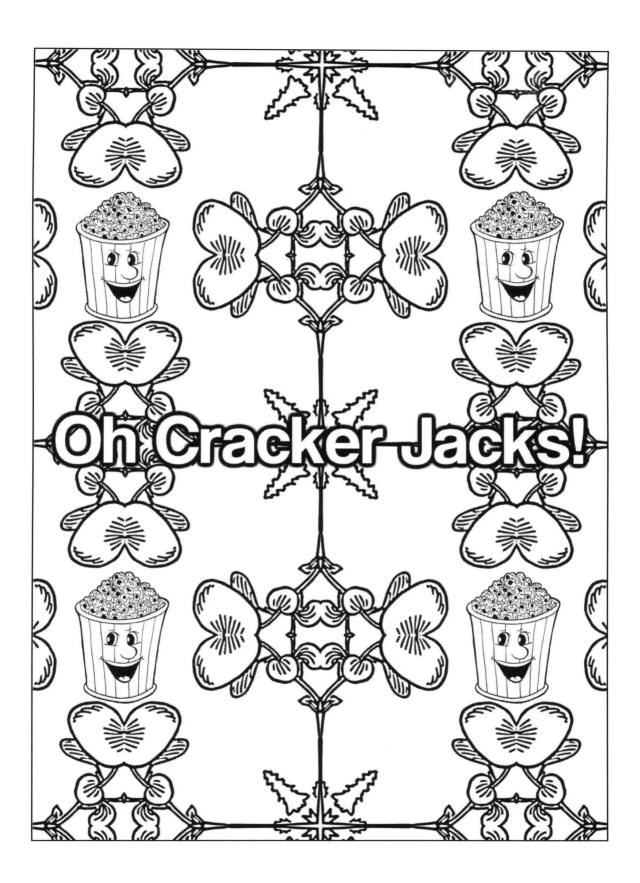

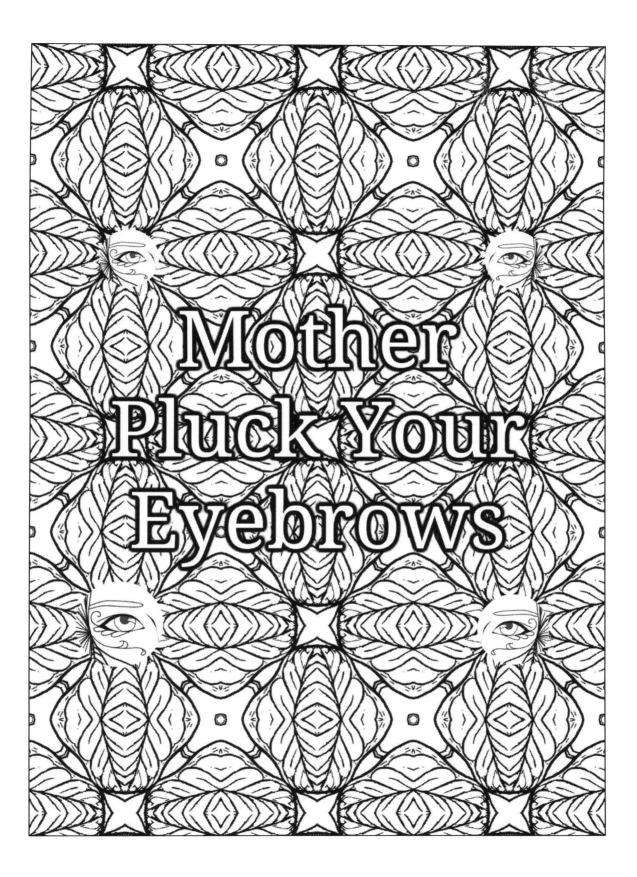

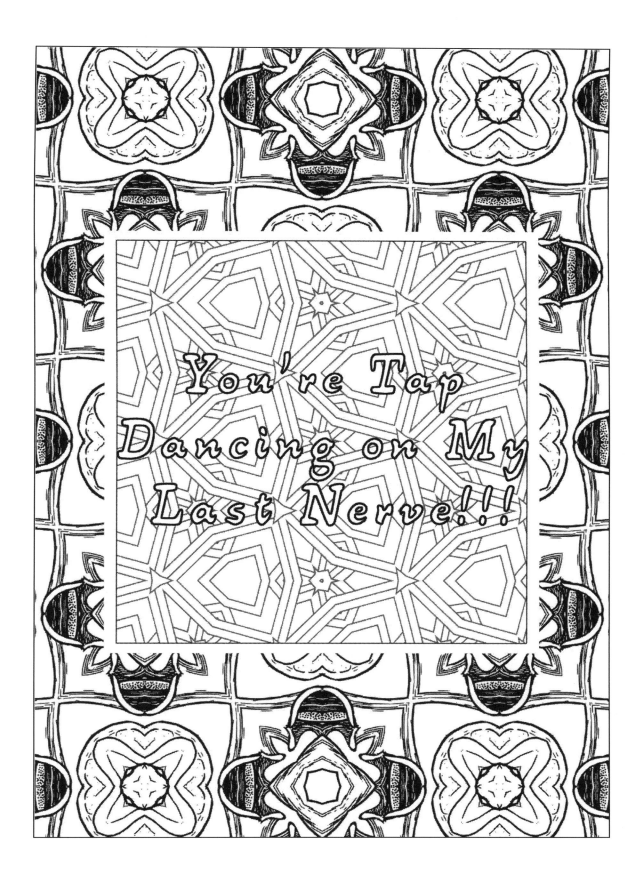

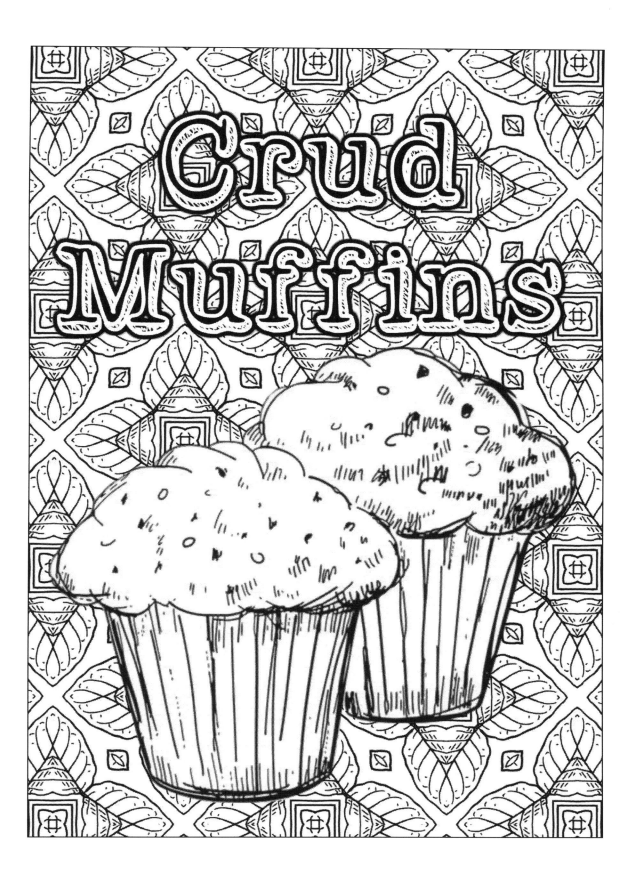

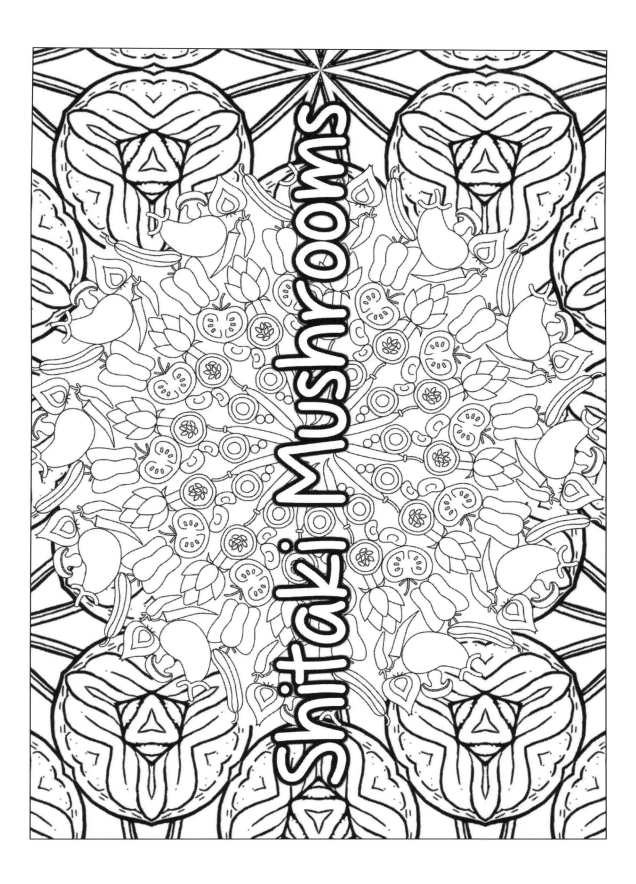

Geez Louise!

i need to use some words that end in *itch and *uck right now

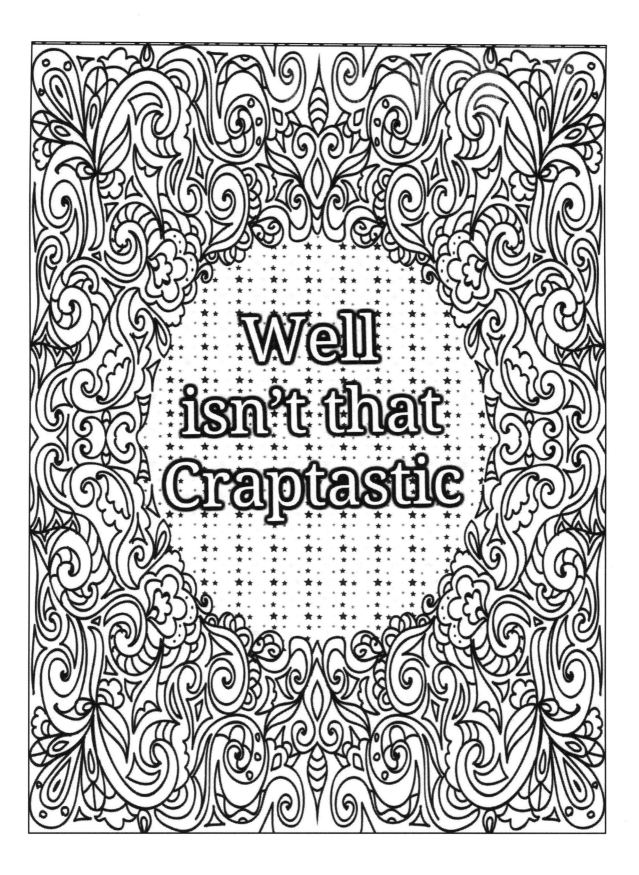

Conclusion

I hope you've enjoyed *Teacher Swears*, and if you did, I'd appreciate it if you would leave a review wherever you bought it – this really helps indie authors and artists like me.

Now if you want to REALLY turn the air blue with some more "colorful" language check out *Southern Swears That'll Get Your Mouth Washed Out with Soap, Mid-Western Swears*, and *Pirate Swears*.

Color me impressed!

I ♥ Coloring Books

18368466R00036

Printed in Great Britain
by Amazon